MW01202041

The Rime of the Ancient Mariner

Progressive School Classics

THE RIME OF THE ANCIENT MARINER

BY

SAMUEL TAYLOR COLERIDGE

Edited with
Biographical Sketch, Portrait, and Notes
by
HELEN WOODROW BONES

CHICAGO
BECKLEY-CARDY COMPANY

The Wedding-Guest sat on a stone:
He cannot choose but hear;
And thus spake on that ancient man,
The bright-eyed Mariner.   20

"The ship was cheered, the harbor cleared;
Merrily did we drop
Below the kirk, below the hill,
Below the lighthouse top.

The Mariner
tells how the
ship sailed
southward
with a good
wind and fair
weather, till it
reached the
Line.

"The sun came up upon the left,   25
Out of the sea came he!
And he shone bright, and on the right
Went down into the sea.

"Higher and higher every day,
Till over the mast at noon—"   30
The Wedding-Guest here beat his breast,
For he heard the loud bassoon.

The Wedding-
Guest heareth
the bridal
music; but the
Mariner con-
tinueth his tale.

The bride hath paced into the hall,
Red as a rose is she;
Nodding their heads before her goes   35
The merry minstrelsy.

The Wedding-Guest he beat his breast,
Yet he cannot choose but hear;
And thus spake on that ancient man
The bright-eyed Mariner.   40

The ship driven
by a storm
toward the
south pole

"And now the Storm-blast came, and he
Was tyrannous and strong:
He struck with his o'ertaking wings,
And chased us south along.

"With sloping masts and dipping prow, 45
As who pursued with yell and blow
Still treads the shadow of his foe,
And forward bends his head,
The ship drove fast, loud roared the blast,
And southward aye we fled. 50

"And now there came both mist and snow,
And it grew wondrous cold:
And ice, mast-high, came floating by,
As green as emerald.

The land of ice,
and of fearful
sounds, where
no living thing
was to be seen

"And through the drifts the snowy clifts 55
Did send a dismal sheen:
Nor shapes of men nor beasts we ken—
The ice was all between.

"The ice was here, the ice was there,
The ice was all around: 60
It cracked and growled, and roared and howled,
Like noises in a swound!

Till a great sea-
bird, called the
Albatross, came
through the
snow-fog, and
was received
with great joy
and hospitality.

"At length did cross an Albatross,
Through the fog it came;
As if it had been a Christian soul, 65
We hailed it in God's name.

"It ate the food it ne'er had eat,
And round and round it flew.
The ice did split with a thunder-fit;
The helmsman steered us through! 70

And lo! the
Albatross
proveth a bird

"And a good south wind sprung up behind;
The Albatross did follow,

of good omen,
and followeth
the ship as it
returned north-
ward through
fog and
floating ice

And every day, for food or play,
Came to the mariners' hollo!

"In mist or cloud, on mast or shroud,   75
It perched for vespers nine;
Whiles all the night, through fog-smoke white,
Glimmered the white moon-shine."

The ancient
Mariner
inhospitably
killeth the
pious bird of
good omen

"God save thee, ancient Mariner!
From the fiends, that plague thee thus!—   80
Why look'st thou so?"—"With my cross-bow
I shot the Albatross!"

PART II

"The Sun now rose upon the right:
Out of the sea came he,
Still hid in mist, and on the left   85
Went down into the sea.

"And the good south wind still blew behind,
But no sweet bird did follow,
Nor any day for food or play
Came to the mariners' hollo!   90

His shipmates
cry out against
the ancient
Mariner, for
killing the bird
of good luck

"And I had done a hellish thing,
And it would work 'em woe:
For all averred, I had killed the bird
That made the breeze to blow.
Ah wretch! said they, the bird to slay,   95
That made the breeze to blow!

But when the
fog cleared off,
they justify the
same, and thus
make them-
selves accom-
plices in the
crime

"Nor dim nor red, like God's own head,
The glorious Sun uprist:
Then all averred, I had killed the bird
That brought the fog and mist.   100

'T was right, said they, such birds to slay,
That bring the fog and mist.

The fair breeze
continues, the
ship enters the
Pacific Ocean,
and sails north-
waid, even till
it reaches the
Line

"The fair breeze blew, the white foam flew,
The furrow followed free;
We were the first that ever burst   105
Into that silent sea.

The ship hath
been suddenly
becalmed

"Down dropt the breeze, the sails dropt down,
'T was sad as sad could be;
And we did speak only to break
The silence of the sea!   110

"All in a hot and copper sky,
The bloody Sun, at noon,
Right up above the mast did stand,
No bigger than the Moon.

"Day after day, day after day,   115
We stuck, nor breath nor motion;
As idle as a painted ship
Upon a painted ocean.

And the Alba-
tross begins to
be avenged.

"Water, water, everywhere,
And all the boards did shrink;   120
Water, water, everywhere,
Nor any drop to drink.

"The very deep did rot: O Christ!
That ever this should be!
Yea, slimy things did crawl with legs   125
Upon the slimy sea.

"About, about, in reel and rout
The death-fires danced at night;

The water, like a witch's oils,
Burnt green, and blue and white.   130

"And some in dreams assurèd were
Of the Spirit that plagued us so;
Nine fathom deep he had followed us
From the land of mist and snow.

"And every tongue, through utter drought,   135
Was withered at the root;
We could not speak, no more than if
We had been choked with soot.

"Ah! well a-day! what evil looks
Had I from old and young!   140
Instead of the cross, the Albatross
About my neck was hung."

PART III

"There passed a weary time. Each throat
Was parched, and glazed each eye.
A weary time! a weary time!   145

How glazed each weary eye,
When looking westward, I beheld
A something in the sky.

"At first it seemed a little speck,
And then it seemed a mist;   150
It moved and moved, and took at last
A certain shape, I wist.

"A speck, a mist, a shape, I wist!
And still it neared and neared:

As if it dodged a water-sprite,   155
It plunged and tacked and veered.

At its nearer
approach, it
seemeth him to
be a ship, and
at a dear ran-
som he freeth
his speech
from the bonds
of thirst.
"With throats unslaked, with black lips baked,
We could nor laugh nor wail;
Through utter drought all dumb we stood!
I bit my arm, I sucked the blood,   160
And cried, 'A sail! a sail!'

"With throats unslaked, with black lips baked,
Agape they heard me call:
A flash of
joy.
Gramercy! they for joy did grin,
And all at once their breath drew in,   165
As they were drinking all.

" 'See! see!' I cried, 'she tacks no more!
And horror
follows. For
can it be a ship
that comes on-
ward without
wind or tide?
Hither to work us weal;
Without a breeze, without a tide,
She steadies with upright keel!'   170

"The western wave was all a-flame:
The day was well nigh done!
Almost upon the western wave
Rested the broad bright Sun;
When that strange shape drove suddenly   175
Betwixt us and the Sun.

It seemeth
him but the
skeleton of
a ship.
"And straight the Sun was flecked with bars,
(Heaven's Mother send us grace!)
As if through a dungeon-grate he peered
With broad and burning face.   180

"Alas (thought I, and my heart beat loud)
How fast she nears and nears!

Are those her sails that glance in the Sun,
Like restless gossameres?

And its ribs are
seen as bars on
the face of the
setting Sun
The Specter-
Woman and
her Death-
mate, and no
other on board
the skeleton-
ship.

"Are those her ribs through which the Sun   185
Did peer, as through a grate?
And is that Woman all her crew?
Is that a Death? and are there two?
Is Death that woman's mate?

Like vessel,
like crew!

"Her lips were red, her looks were free,   190
Her locks were yellow as gold:
Her skin was as white as leprosy,
The Night-mare Life-in-Death was she,
Who thicks man's blood with cold.

Death and
Life-in-Death
have diced for
the ship's
crew, and she
(the latter)
winneth the
ancient
Mariner

"The naked hulk alongside came,   195
And the twain were casting dice;
'The game is done! I've won! I've won!'
Quoth she, and whistles thrice.

No twilight
within the
courts of the
Sun

"The Sun's rim dips; the stars rush out:
At one stride comes the dark;   200
With far-heard whisper, o'er the sea,
Off shot the specter-bark.

At the rising
of the Moon,

"We listened and looked sideways up!
Fear at my heart, as at a cup,
My life-blood seemed to sip!   205
The stars were dim, and thick the night,
The steersman's face by his lamp gleamed white;
From the sails the dew did drip—
Till clomb above the eastern bar
The hornèd Moon, with one bright star   210
Within the nether tip.

"One after one, by the star-dogged Moon,
Too quick for groan or sigh,
Each turned his face with a ghastly pang,
And cursed me with his eye. 215

"Four times fifty living men,
(And I heard nor sigh nor groan)
With heavy thump, a lifeless lump,
They dropped down one by one.

"The souls did from their bodies fly,— 220
They fled to bliss or woe!
And every soul, it passed me by,
Like the whizz of my cross-bow!"

PART IV

"I fear thee, ancient Mariner!
I fear thy skinny hand! 225
And thou art long, and lank, and brown,
As is the ribbed sea-sand.

"I fear thee and thy glittering eye,
And thy skinny hand, so brown."—

"Fear not, fear not, thou Wedding-Guest! 230
This body dropt not down.

"Alone, alone, all, all alone,
Alone on a wide, wide sea!
And never a saint took pity on
My soul in agony. 235

"The many men, so beautiful!
And they all dead did lie:
And a thousand thousand slimy things
Lived on; and so did I.

And envieth
that they
should live,
and so many
lie dead.

"I looked upon the rotting sea,   240
And drew my eyes away;
I looked upon the rotting deck,
And there the dead men lay.

"I looked to heaven, and tried to pray;
But or ever a prayer had gusht,   245
A wicked whisper came, and made
My heart as dry as dust.

"I closed my lids, and kept them close,
And the balls like pulses beat;
For the sky and the sea, and the sea and the sky   250
Lay like a load on my weary eye,
And the dead were at my feet.

But the curse
liveth for him
in the eye of
the dead men

"The cold sweat melted from their limbs,
Nor rot nor reek did they:
The look with which they looked on me   255
Had never passed away.

"An orphan's curse would drag to hell
A spirit from on high;
But oh! more horrible than that
Is a curse in a dead man's eye!   260
Seven days, seven nights, I saw that curse,
And yet I could not die.

In his loneli-
ness and fixed-
ness he yearn-
eth towards the
journeying
Moon, and the
stars that still
sojourn, yet
still move on-
ward, and
everywhere
the blue sky
belongs to
them, and is
their appointed

"The moving Moon went up the sky,
And no where did abide:
Softly she was going up,   265
And a star or two beside—

"Her beams bemocked the sultry main,
Like April hoar-frost spread;

rest, and their native country and their own natural homes, which they enter unannounced, as lords that are certainly expected, and yet there is a silent joy at their arrival.

But where the ship's huge shadow lay,
The charmèd water burnt alway   270
A still and awful red.

By the light of the Moon he beholdeth God's creatures of the great calm

"Beyond the shadow of the ship,
I watched the water-snakes:
They moved in tracks of shining white,
And when they reared, the elfish light   275
Fell off in hoary flakes.

"Within the shadow of the ship
I watched their rich attire:
Blue, glossy green, and velvet black,
They coiled and swam; and every track   280
Was a flash of golden fire.

Their beauty and their happiness

"O happy living things! no tongue
Their beauty might declare:
A spring of love gushed from my heart,

He blesseth them in his heart.

And I blessed them unaware!   285
Sure my kind saint took pity on me
And I blessed them unaware.

The spell begins to break.

"The selfsame moment I could pray;
And from my neck so free
The Albatross fell off, and sank   290
Like lead into the sea."

PART V

"Oh sleep! it is a gentle thing,
Beloved from pole to pole!
To Mary Queen the praise be given!
She sent the gentle sleep from Heaven,   295
That slid into my soul.

"The silly buckets on the deck,
That had so long remained,
I dreamt that they were filled with dew;
And when I awoke, it rained.   300

"My lips were wet, my throat was cold,
My garments all were dank;
Sure I had drunken in my dreams,
And still my body drank.

"I moved, and could not feel my limbs: 305
I was so light—almost
I thought that I had died in sleep,
And was a blessed ghost.

"And soon I heard a roaring wind:
It did not come anear;   310
But with its sound it shook the sails,
That were so thin and sere.

"The upper air burst into life!
And a hundred fire-flags sheen,
To and fro they were hurried about!   315
And to and fro, and in and out,
The wan stars danced between.

"And the coming wind did roar more loud,
And the sails did sigh like sedge;
And the rain poured down from one black cloud; 320
The Moon was at its edge.

"The thick black cloud was cleft, and still
The Moon was at its side:
Like waters shot from some high crag,

The lightning fell with never a jag,   325
A river steep and wide.

The bodies of
the ship's crew
are inspired,
and the ship
moves on,
"The loud wind never reached the ship,
Yet now the ship moved on!
Beneath the lightning and the Moon
The dead men gave a groan.   330

"They groaned, they stirred, they all uprose,
Nor spake, nor moved their eyes;
It had been strange, even in a dream,
To have seen those dead men rise.

"The helmsman steered, the ship moved on;   335
Yet never a breeze up blew;
The mariners all 'gan work the ropes,
Where they were wont to do;
They raised their limbs like lifeless tools—
We were a ghastly crew.   340

"The body of my brother's son
Stood by me, knee to knee:
The body and I pulled at one rope,
But he said nought to me."

But not by the
souls of the
men, nor by
demons of
earth or middle
air, but by a
blessed troop of
angelic spirits,
sent down by
the invocation
of the guardian
saint.
"I fear thee, ancient Mariner!"   345
"Be calm, thou Wedding-Guest!
'T was not those souls that fled in pain,
Which to their corses came again,
But a troop of spirits blest:

"For when it dawned—they dropped their arms, 350
And clustered round the mast;
Sweet sounds rose slowly through their mouths,
And from their bodies passed.

"Around, around, flew each sweet sound,
Then darted to the Sun;   355
Slowly the sounds came back again,
Now mixed, now one by one.

"Sometimes a-dropping from the sky
I heard the skylark sing;
Sometimes all little birds that are,   360
How they seemed to fill the sea and air
With their sweet jargoning!

"And now 't was like all instruments,
Now like a lonely flute;
And now it is an angel's song,   365
That makes the heavens be mute.

"It ceased; yet still the sails made on
A pleasant noise till noon,
A noise like of a hidden brook
In the leafy month of June,   370
That to the sleeping woods all night
Singeth a quiet tune.

"Till noon we quietly sailed on,
Yet never a breeze did breathe:
Slowly and smoothly went the ship,   ·   375
Moved onward from beneath.

The lonesome
Spirit from the
south pole
carries on the
ship as far as
the Line, in
obedience to
the angelic
troop, but still
requireth
vengeance

"Under the keel nine fathom deep,
From the land of mist and snow,
The spirit slid: and it was he
That made the ship to go.   380
The sails at noon left off their tune,
And the ship stood still also.

"The Sun, right up above the mast,
Had fixed her to the ocean:
But in a minute she 'gan stir,   385
With a short uneasy motion—
Backwards and forwards half her length,
With a short uneasy motion.

"Then like a pawing horse let go,
She made a sudden bound: 390
It flung the blood into my head,
And I fell down in a swound.

The Polar Spirit's fellow demons, the invisible inhabitants of the element, take part in his wrong, and two of them relate, one to the other, that penance long and heavy for the ancient Mariner hath been accorded to the Polar Spirit, who returneth southward.

"How long in that same fit I lay,
I have not to declare;
But ere my living life returned,   395
I heard, and in my soul discerned,
Two voices in the air.

" 'Is it he?' quoth one, 'is this the man?
By him who died on cross,
With his cruel bow he laid full low   400
The harmless Albatross.

" 'The Spirit who bideth by himself
In the land of mist and snow,
He loved the bird that loved the man
Who shot him with his bow.'   405

"The other was a softer voice,
As soft as honey-dew:
Quoth he, 'The man hath penance done,
And penance more will do.' "

PART VI

FIRST VOICE

" 'But tell me, tell me! speak again,   410
Thy soft response renewing—
What makes that ship drive on so fast?
What is the Ocean doing?'

SECOND VOICE

" 'Still as a slave before his lord,
The Ocean hath no blast,   415
His great bright eye most silently
Up to the Moon is cast—

" 'If he may know which way to go;
For she guides him smooth or grim.
See, brother, see! how graciously   420
She looketh down on him.'

FIRST VOICE

The Mariner hath been cast into a trance, for the angelic power causeth the vessel to drive northward, faster than human life could endure

" 'But why drives on that ship so fast,
Without or wave or wind?'

SECOND VOICE

" 'The air is cut away before,
And closes from behind.'   425

" 'Fly, brother, fly! more high, more high!
Or we shall be belated:
For slow and slow that ship will go,
When the Mariner's trance is abated.'

The supernatural motion is retarded, the Mariner

"I woke, and we were sailing on   430
As in a gentle weather:

awakes, and
his penance
begins anew

'T was night, calm night, the moon was high,
The dead men stood together.

"All stood together on the deck,
For a charnel-dungeon fitter: 435
All fixed on me their stony eyes,
That in the Moon did glitter.

"The pang, the curse, with which they died,
Had never passed away:
I could not draw my eyes from theirs,   440
Nor turn them up to pray.

The curse is
finally
expiated

"And now this spell was snapt; once more
I viewed the ocean green,
And looked far forth, yet little saw
Of what had else been seen—   445

"Like one, that on a lonesome road
Doth walk in fear and dread,
And having once turned round, walks on,
And turns no more his head;
Because he knows, a frightful fiend   450
Doth close behind him tread.

"But soon there breathed a wind on me,
Nor sound nor motion made:
Its path was not upon the sea,
In ripple or in shade.   455

"It raised my hair, it fanned my cheek
Like a meadow-gale of spring—
It mingled strangely with my fears,
Yet it felt like a welcoming

"Swiftly, swiftly flew the ship,   460
Yet she sailed softly too:
Sweetly, sweetly blew the breeze—
On me alone it blew.

And the an-
cient Mariner
beholdeth
his native
country.

"Oh! dream of joy! is this indeed
The lighthouse top I see?   465
Is this the hill? is this the kirk?
Is this mine own countree?

"We drifted o'er the harbor-bar,
And I with sobs did pray—
'O let me be awake, my God!   470
Or let me sleep alway.'

"The harbor-bay was clear as glass,
So smoothly it was strewn!
And on the bay the moonlight lay,
And the shadow of the Moon.   .   475

"The rock shone bright, the kirk no less,
That stands above the rock:
The moonlight steeped in silentness
The steady weathercock.

"And the bay was white with silent light   480
Till, rising from the same,

The angelic
spirits leave
the dead
bodies.

Full many shapes, that shadows were,
In crimson colors came.

And appear
in their own
forms of light

"A little distance from the prow
Those crimson shadows were: 485
I turned my eyes upon the deck—
Oh, Christ! what saw I there!

"Each corse lay flat, lifeless and flat,
And, by the holy rood!
A man all light, a seraph-man,   490
On every corse there stood.

"This seraph-band, each waved his hand:
It was a heavenly sight!
They stood as signals to the land,
Each one a lovely light;   495

"This seraph-band, each waved his hand,
No voice did they impart—
No voice; but oh! the silence sank
Like music on my heart.

"But soon I heard the dash of oars,   500
I heard the Pilot's cheer;
My head was turned perforce away,
And I saw a boat appear.

"The Pilot and the Pilot's boy,
I heard them coming fast: 505
Dear Lord in Heaven! it was a joy
The dead men could not blast.

"I saw a third—I heard his voice:
It is the Hermit good!
He singeth loud his goodly hymns   510
That he makes in the wood
He'll shrieve my soul, he'll wash away
The Albatross's blood.

PART VII

"This Hermit good lives in that wood
Which slopes down to the sea.　　　　　　515
How loudly his sweet voice he rears!
He loves to talk with marineres
That come from a far countree.

"He kneels at morn, and noon, and eve—
He hath a cushion plump:　　　　　　520
It is the moss that wholly hides
The rotted old oak-stump.

"The skiff-boat neared: I heard them talk,
'Why, this is strange, I trow!
Where are those lights so many and fair,　　　525
That signal made but now?'

" 'Strange, by my faith!' the Hermit said—
'And they answered not our cheer!
The planks looked warped! and see those sails,
How thin they are and sere!　　　　　　530
I never saw aught like to them,
Unless perchance it were

" 'Brown skeletons of leaves that lag
My forest-brook along;
When the ivy-tod is heavy with snow,　　　535
And the owlet whoops to the wolf below,
That eats the she-wolf's young.'

" 'Dear Lord! it hath a fiendish look'—
(The Pilot made reply,)
'I am a-feared'—'Push on, push on!'　　　540
Said the Hermit cheerily.

"The boat came closer to the ship,
But I nor spake nor stirred;
The boat came close beneath the ship,
And straight a sound was heard. 545

The ship
suddenly
sinketh

"Under the water it rumbled on,
Still louder and more dread:
It reached the ship, it split the bay,
The ship went down like lead.

The ancient
Mariner is
saved in the
Pilot's boat

"Stunned by that loud and dreadful sound, 550
Which sky and ocean smote,
Like one that hath been seven days drowned,
My body lay afloat;
But swift as dreams, myself I found
Within the Pilot's boat. 555

"Upon the whirl, where sank the ship,
The boat spun round and round;
And all was still, save that the hill
Was telling of the sound.

"I moved my lips—the Pilot shrieked, 560
And fell down in a fit;
The holy Hermit raised his eyes,
And prayed where he did sit.

"I took the oars: the Pilot's boy,
Who now doth crazy go, 565
Laughed loud and long, and all the while
His eyes went to and fro.
'Ha! ha!' quoth he, 'full plain I see,
The Devil knows how to row.'

"And now, all in my own countree,   570
I stood on the firm land!
The Hermit stepped forth from the boat,
And scarcely he could stand.

The ancient
Mariner ear-
nestly entreat-
eth the Hermit
to shrieve
him; and the
penance of life
falls on him.

" 'O shrieve me, shrieve me, holy man!'
The Hermit crossed his brow.   575
'Say quick,' quoth he, 'I bid thee say—
What manner of man art thou?'

"Forthwith this frame of mine was wrenched
With a woful agony,
Which forced me to begin my tale;   580
And then it left me free.

And ever and
anon through-
out his future
life an agony
constraineth
him to travel
from land to
land.

"Since then, at an uncertain hour,
That agony returns:
And till my ghastly tale is told,
This heart within me burns.   585

"I pass, like night, from land to land;
I have strange power of speech;
That moment that his face I see,
I know the man that must hear me:
To him my tale I teach.   590

"What loud uproar bursts from that door!
The wedding-guests are there;
But in the garden-bower the bride
And bride-maids singing are:
And hark the little vesper bell,   595
Which biddeth me to prayer!

"O Wedding-Guest! this soul hath been
Alone on a wide, wide sea:

So lonely 't was, that God himself
Scarce seemed there to be.   600

"O sweeter than the marriage-feast,
'T is sweeter far to me,
To walk together to the kirk
With a goodly company!—

"To walk together to the kirk,   605
And all together pray,
While each to his great Father bends
Old men, and babes, and loving friends,
And youths and maidens gay!

And to teach,
by his own
example, love
and reverence
to all things
that God made
and loveth.

"Farewell, farewell! but this I tell   610
To thee, thou Wedding-Guest!
He prayeth well, who loveth well
Both man and bird and beast.

"He prayeth best, who loveth best
All things both great and small;   615
For the dear God who loveth us,
He made and loveth all."

The Mariner, whose eye is bright,
Whose beard with age is hoar,
Is gone: and now the Wedding-Guest   620
Turned from the bridegroom's door.

He went like one that hath been stunned,
And is of sense forlorn:
A sadder and a wiser man,
He rose the morrow morn.   625

NOTES

[The numbers refer to lines in the text]

In 1765 Bishop Percy published his "Reliques of Ancient English Poetry"—a collection of old ballads once popular in England, but in danger of being quite forgotten because not preserved in print. His book was received with such interest as to create anew a taste for those quaint verse-stories, composed in the olden days partly by the people themselves and partly by the minstrels who wandered from place to place, singing and reciting the traditional history of their land. This ballad-revival inspired many poets of the time to try their hand at ballad-writing. Among those who felt the keenest interest in the revival were Coleridge and his close friend William Wordsworth, who published in 1798 a volume entitled "Lyrical Ballads." The purpose and scope of this work are stated in Coleridge's "Biographia Literaria" (Chapter XIV):

"During the first year that Mr. Wordsworth and I were neighbours, our conversations turned frequently on the two cardinal points of poetry, the power of exciting the sympathy of the reader by a faithful adherence to the truth of nature, and the power of giving the interest of novelty by the modifying colours of imagination. The sudden charm, which accidents of light and shade, which moonlight or sunset, diffused over a known and familiar landscape, appeared to represent the practicability of combining both. These are the poetry of nature. The thought suggested itself (to which of us I do not recollect) that a series of poems might be composed of two sorts. In the one, the incidents and agents were to be, in part at least, supernatural; and the excellence aimed at was to consist in the interesting of the affections by the dramatic truth of such emotions, as would naturally accompany such situations, supposing them real. And real in this sense they have been to every human being who, from whatever source of delusion, has at any time believed himself under supernatural agency. For the second class, subjects were to be chosen from ordinary life; the characters and incidents were to be such as will be found in every village and its vicinity where there is a meditative and feeling mind to seek after them, or to notice them when they present themselves.

"In this idea originated the plan of the 'Lyrical Ballads,' in which it was agreed that my endeavours should be directed to persons and characters supernatural, or at least romantic; yet so as to transfer from our inward nature a human interest and a semblance of truth sufficient to procure for these shadows of imagination that willing suspension of disbelief for the moment, which constitutes poetic faith. Mr. Wordsworth, on the other hand, was to propose to himself as his object, to give the charm of novelty to things of every day, and to excite a feeling analogous to the supernatural, by awakening the mind's attention from the lethargy of custom, and directing it to the loveliness and wonders of the world before us; an inexhaustible treasure, but for which, in consequence of the film of familiarity and selfish solicitude, we have eyes, yet see not, ears that hear not, and hearts that neither feel nor understand.

"With this view I wrote 'The Ancient Mariner.'"

The immediate cause for the writing of this poem has been told by Wordsworth, who in the autumn of 1798, with his sister and Coleridge, took a walking-trip to Linton and the Valley of Stones: "As our united funds were very small, we agreed to defray the expense of the tour by writing a poem, to be sent to the *New Monthly Magazine*. Accordingly we set off . . . and in the course of this walk was planned the poem of 'The Ancient Mariner.' . . . We began the composition together on that, to me, memorable evening. . . As we endeavoured to proceed conjointly (I speak of the same evening) our respective manners proved so widely different that it would have been quite presumptuous in me to do anything but separate from an undertaking upon which I could only have been a clog. . . 'The Ancient Mariner' grew and grew till it became too important for our first object, which was limited to our expectation of five pounds; and we began to think of a volume, which was to consist, as Mr. Coleridge has told the world, of poems chiefly on supernatural subjects, taken from common life, but looked at, as much as might be, through an imaginative medium."

"The Rime of the Ancyent Marinere, In Seven Parts," appeared anonymously in "Lyrical Ballads" the following year. While not a ballad in the strictest sense of the word, the poem carries out the ballad idea in its structure and details; in the extreme simplicity of its style and diction, and in the employment of devices common to ballad poetry. These last are pointed out as they occur, in the notes which follow. As it originally appeared, it was full of archaic words, phrases, and spellings, most of which were discarded by the poet later, and comprised a number of stanzas he afterward omitted. It is not to our purpose to consider all his changes: the poem is given here as he left it after many thorough revisions.

Rime: rhyme. The former spelling is correct, etymologically, and is now used by many writers in place of the latter.

Facile credo, etc. This motto, from Thomas Burnet's "Archælogiæ Philosophicæ," prefaced the poem for the first time in "Sibylline Leaves," in 1817. In the Mead and Toxton edition of 1736 the translation is given thus: "I can easily believe that there are more Invisible than Visible beings in the Universe. But who will declare to us the family of all these, and acquaint us with the Agreements, Differences, and peculiar Talents which are to be found among them? . . . It is true, Human Wit has always desired a knowledge of these things, though it has never yet attained it. I will own that it is very profitable, sometimes to contemplate in the Mind, as in a Draught, the Image of the greater and better World; lest the Soul, being accustomed to the Trifles of this present Life, should contract itself too much, and altogether rest in mean Cogitations; but, in the mean Time, we must take Care to keep to the Truth, and observe Moderation, that we may distinguish Certain from Uncertain Things, and Day from Night."

Glosses. As the poem originally appeared, there were no marginal readings, these being added in 1817. In the first edition the poem was preceded by an Argument, which in the second was a good deal enlarged and read thus: "How a Ship having first sailed to the Equator, was driven by storms, to the cold Country towards the South Pole; how the Ancient Mariner, cruelly, and in contempt of the laws of hospitality, killed a Sea-bird; and how he was followed by many strange Judgments; and in what manner he came back to his own Country." After the second edition this Argument was discarded altogether by the poet.

1. It is. This abrupt form of introduction—in which the speaker is merely suggested—is found in many of the old ballads.

2. one of three. Note how much more effective the tale is made by the part played by the Wedding-Guest, with his unwillingness to listen; the fascination the Ancient Mariner gains over him, until he is fairly spellbound; his occasional interruptions, showing the effect upon him of the old man's words and appearance.

5. The Bridegroom's doors, etc. The weirdness of the Mariner's tale is heightened by the references, here and there, to the natural, commonplace details of the wedding.

8. May'st hear, etc. "Thou" is understood here. The dropping of the subject emphasizes the impatience of the Wedding-Guest to be gone.

9-20. He holds, etc. Note the effectiveness of the contrast between the merriment of the wedding-feast and the horror the Mariner excites in the Wedding-Guest.

12. Eftsoons (from the Anglo-Saxon words *aeft*, afterward, and *sona*, soon): immediately, forthwith. (Archaic.)

15-16. And listens, etc. Wordsworth suggested these two lines.

21-50. The ship was cheered, etc. William Watson, in his "Excursions in Criticism," says: "There is perhaps something rather inartistic in his undignified haste to convey us to the æsthetically necessary region. In some half-dozen stanzas, beginning with 'The ship was cleared,' we find ourselves crossing the line and driven far towards the Southern Pole." This very haste in the narrative, like the abruptness with which the old man begins his tale (line 10), indicates the narrator's intense earnestness and the necessity he feels of telling his story at once after he has gained the attention of the Wedding-Guest (from line 21 on).

22. drop: sail toward the sea.

23. kirk: church. This dialect word, used to carry out the ballad idea, is not really appropriate here, as we see later that the Mariner is a Roman Catholic and as such he would hardly have used the word.

25. upon the left. That is, the ship was sailing south.

30. over the mast at noon. At what point would the sun be directly above the ship at noon, as he is about to describe it?

35. Nodding their heads. But the singular form of the verb is used. This lack of agreement, like the lack of coherence of tenses, is characteristic of ballad poetry.

36. minstrelsy: musicians.

39-40. And thus, etc. See lines 19 and 20. This sort of repetition is a device common to the old ballads.

40. The bright-eyed Mariner. Notice how vivid a picture is given merely by the use of such phrases as "long gray beard," "glittering eye," "skinny hand," "gray-beard loon," "bright-eyed Mariner." No detailed description of "the ancient man" could have given us a clearer picture of him.

41. Storm-blast. There are several of these pleonastic compounds in the poem. Storm and blast are one and the same here.

46. As who pursued. "One" and "is" are understood here.

47. Still: constantly. **Treads the shadow of his foe** conveys the idea of being very closely followed. Supposing the pursuer to be between the pursued and the sun, his shadow would extend toward the pursued, who could not be touched by it unless the pursuer were close upon him.

55. drifts: drifting clouds of mist. **clifts:** cliffs; that is, icebergs.

57. ken: see.

62. swound: swoon; faint. (Archaic.)

63. Albatross. Wordsworth tells us that he himself suggested to Coleridge the killing of the albatross. He says: "Some crime was to be committed which should bring upon the old navigator, as Coleridge always delighted to call him, the spectral persecution, as a consequence of that crime, and his own wanderings. I had been reading in Shelvock's *Voyages* a day or two before, that while doubling Cape Horn they frequently saw albatrosses in that latitude, the largest of sea fowl, some extending their wings twelve or fifteen feet. 'Suppose,' said I, 'you represent him as having killed one of these birds upon entering the South Sea, and that the tutelary spirits of those regions take upon them to avenge the crime?' The incident was thought fit for the purpose and adopted accordingly."

64. thorough. In olden times the same word as "through." We meet with it frequently in Shakespeare and other early English poets.

67. eat (pronounced *et*): eaten. Now archaic as the past participle of the verb "to eat."

76. vespers: literally, the hour of evening prayer in the Roman Catholic Church. Here the expression means, simply, "evenings."

77. Whiles. Archaic form of "while." **fog-smoke.** See note on line 41.

79. God save thee. See note on line 2. This interruption greatly intensifies the gruesomeness of the Mariner's tale.

83. The Sun now rose upon the right because the ship was sailing north. See line 25.

97. Nor . . . nor: neither . nor. "But" is understood before like. **Head** is used here for "face." See Matt. XVII. 2., and Rev. I. 16.

98. uprist. In olden times commonly used for "uprose."

104. followed free. This is the original reading. In a later edition the poet made it "streamed off free," saying of the other phrase: "I had not been long on board a ship before I perceived that this was the image as seen by the spectator from the shore, or from another vessel." Later, however, he restored the original reading.

125. slimy things. Coleridge had used this idea in his "Destiny of Nations":

As what time after long and pestful calms,
With slimy shapes and miscreated life
Poisoning the vast Pacific, etc

128. death-fires. Perhaps the reference is to the phosphorescent lights to be seen at sea on the surface of the water and in the rigging of vessels; but probably he meant similar lights which once were supposed to appear over dead bodies, or in houses where a death was to occur. In his "Ode on the Departing Year" we read:

Mighty armies of the dead
Dance, like death-fires, round her tomb.

129. like a witch's oils. Oils, that is, which burn with a weird and lurid light.

131. Gloss. Josephus: a noted Jewish historian who lived in the first century A. D. **Michael Sellus** was a Byzantine philosopher of the eleventh century, among whose writings is a "Dialogue on the Operation of Demons."

142. About my neck. Notice that Parts I, II, IV, and VI end with an allusion to the albatross

152. I wist. Wist means "know." Coleridge uses **I wist** here, however, in the sense of "iwis," an archaic word meaning "certainly."

164. Gramercy (from the Old French *grand merci*, many thanks) is used here, as often in early English poetry, merely as an exclamation of surprise, not as an expression of gratitude.

169. without a breeze. The idea of a phantom ship is, of course, not original with Coleridge; we have it in the story of the Flying Dutchman and various other tales, ancient and modern. Wordsworth tells us that Coleridge patterned his after one seen by a friend of his in a dream. But, wherever he got the idea, his phantom ship is quite different from those of other stories.

178. Heaven's Mother: the Virgin Mary See note on line 23.

184. gossameres: fine cobwebs.

185. her ribs. The first and second editions of "The Ancient Mariner" had the two following stanzas here·

> Are those her naked ribs, which fleck'd
> The sun that did behind them peer?
> And are those two all, all the crew,
> That woman and her fleshless Pheere?
>
> His bones are black with many a crack,
> All black and bare, I ween;
> Jet-black and bare, save where with rust
> Of mouldy damps and charnel crust
> They 're patched with purple and green

197. I've won! Life-in-Death wins the Ancient Mariner, while the rest of the crew belong to Death

198. thrice. Three is one of the mystical numbers used in charms. The student will recall the witches' incantations in "Macbeth":

> Thrice to thine, and thrice to mine.
> And thrice again to make up nine —
> Peace'—the charm's wound up

In the first edition this stanza (lines 195-198) was followed by:

> A gust of wind sterte up behind
> And whistled thro' his bones,
> Thro' the holes of his eyes and the hole of his mouth,
> Half-whistles and half-groans.

199. Gloss. courts of the Sun. That is, the tropics.

200. At one stride. Any one who has been in tropical or semitropical countries can appreciate the aptness of this expression.

209. clomb: climbed. (Archaic.)

210-211. one bright star, etc. Originally this read "almost atween the tips," but later the poet substituted the reading given here, adding this note: "It is a common superstition among sailors that something evil is about to happen whenever a star dogs the moon." James Dykes Campbell gives this note in his edition of Coleridge's poems, with the comment. "But no sailor ever saw a star within the nether tip of a horned moon."

222-223. every soul, etc. It was once believed that the soul might be heard leaving the body of a person who had just died.

223. my cross-bow. The mention of this weapon places the date of the Mariner's story before the sixteenth century, as cross-bows were not used later.

224-229. I fear thee. See notes on lines 2 and 79 "With what consummate art are we left to imagine the physical traces which the Mariner's long agony had left behind it, by a method far more terrible than any direct description—the effect, namely, which the sight of him produces upon others.—*Traill's "Life of Coleridge."*

226-227. And thou art long, etc. Wordsworth suggested these two lines.

245. or ere: ere, before. (Archaic.)

261. seven days, seven nights. Seven, like three, has always been considered a mystic number

273. water-snakes. Brandl tells us that Coleridge seems to have taken great interest in such reptiles, his notebook covering the period in which he wrote "The Ancient Mariner" having contained "long paragraphs upon the alligators, boas, and crocodiles of antediluvian times."

285. I blessed them. His hard, rebellious heart is softened and immediately the curse is diminished.

290-291. The Albatross fell off, etc. This is the turning-point of the story.

294. Mary Queen: the Virgin Mary. See note on line 23.

297. silly: frail, weak; here, useless.

314. fire-flags. A reference, undoubtedly, to the Northern Lights Hearne wrote in 1795. "In still nights I have frequently heard them make a rustling and crackling noise, like the waving of a large flag in a fresh gale of wind." Coleridge, who is known to have read Hearne's book, may have had this description in mind. **sheen** is used here, as once commonly, as an adjective to mean "bright" See line 56.

349-366. a troop of spirits blest. Contrast this with the previous description of the dead men, lines 331-344.

407. honey-dew: a sweet, sticky substance found on plants, supposed to be the food of fairies.

435. charnel-dungeon: a vault in which dead bodies are placed

464-467. dream of joy! See lines 21-24

467. countree. This archaic form of "country" is frequently used in ballads.

472. Harbor-bay. See note on line 41.

489. rood: cross. By "holy rood," of course, is meant the cross on which Christ was crucified. In olden times it was not considered wrong to swear by sacred objects and names.

512. shrieve (shrive): to hear confession and grant absolution.

523. skiff-boat. See note on line 41.

524. trow: think

535. ivy-tod: ivy bush or clump of ivy. (Dialect.)

560-569. the Pilot shrieked. See note on lines 224-229.

575. crossed his brow. That is, made upon it the sign of the cross, to avert any evil influence which the Mariner might seek to exert. See note on line 23 and line 294.

582-590. since then, etc We have seen how (lines 287-291) the curse was diminished, but as the spirit said (in lines 408-409), the Mariner must continue to do penance for his sin. **I know the man, etc.** See line 18.

591-596. What loud uproar, etc. The same device of contrast is used here—to heighten the effect of the Mariner's words—as was used in the opening stanzas of the poem. See note on lines 9-20.

612-617. He prayeth well, etc A friend of the poet once told him that she admired "The Ancient Mariner" very much, but that it had two faults—it was improbable and it had no moral. "As for the probability," Coleridge says, "I owned that that might admit some question; but as to the want of a moral, I told her that in my own judgment the poem had too much; and that the only, or chief fault, if I might say so, was the obtrusion of the moral sentiment so openly on the reader as a principle or cause of action in a work of such pure imagination. It ought to have had no more moral than the Arabian Nights' tale of the merchant's sitting down to eat dates by the side of a well, and throwing the shells aside, and lo! a genie starts up, and says he *must* kill the aforesaid merchant, *because* one of the date shells had, it seems, put out the eye of the genie's son."— *Table Talk.*

623. of sense forlorn: bereft of his senses.

LANGUAGE AND COMPOSITION BY GRADES

—————————A HANDBOOK FOR TEACHERS—————————

Covering the Eight Grades of Elementary Schools

By J. M. Hammond
Principal of Morse School, Pittsburgh, Pa.

THIS new work should be in the hands of every elementary school teacher, and if so, would go a long way toward meeting the need of ready expression in both oral and written language. The author believes that if the pupil can be made to feel natural, whatever ideas he has will be freely expressed, and with this in view has prepared a series of type lessons in language and composition which are bound to revolutionize the teaching of this subject in the average schoolroom.

The book follows well established pedagogical principles and is divided into nine parts: one for each of the eight grades, and the last a review of the year's work by grades. The material has been carefully graded, and more than enough has been presented to cover each year's requirements. Much of it has been tried successfully in the schoolroom, and is therefore offered with confidence that the results will prove most satisfactory.

The necessity for the frequent review of language principles and practice is one reason for combining the eight-years' course in one volume. Under this arrangement, the teacher will have ready access to what is offered in the other grades, and will therefore not be compelled to search continually for supplementary work. Beginning with exercises designed to set the young learner at his ease, the work is carried along from grade to grade, with proper and frequent reviews, until he has finished the eight years, equipped with a good working knowledge of expression that should fit him for entrance into the high school, or for embarking upon whatever business he may choose. Present-day methods call for *less technical grammar and more actual practice* in correct forms, with the statement of principles on which correct usage is based, and the author has borne that fact in mind throughout the work.

308 pages. Fully indexed. Cloth. Price, 85 cents

BECKLEY-CARDY COMPANY   Publishers   **CHICAGO**

BEST BOOKS AND HEL[...]

——————————— OF ALL GRA[...]

Morning Exercises for All the Year. [...] of the "Nixie Bunny" books, etc. [...] over 300 exercises, arranged day by day, there being an exercise for each morning of the ten school months, beginning with the first day in September and ending with the last day in June. 252 large pages. Cloth. Price, 60 cents.

Language Games for All Grades. By Alhambra G. Deming, Principal Washington School, Winona, Minn. Designed to establish the habit of correct speech and to increase the child's vocabulary. 90 pages. Cloth. Price (with 53 cards for pupils' use), 65 cents.

Easy Things to Draw. By D. R. Augsburg. A teacher's handbook, with 203 simple drawings for reproducing on the blackboard. 77 large pages. Paper. Price, 30 cents.

Simplex Class Record. The most convenient, compact and practical teacher's class book published. Provides space for 432 names. 76 pages, ruled in three colors. Size, 4½x7¾ inches. Cloth. Price, 30 cents.

Simplex Seat Plan. A simple card and pocket device for keeping a correct list of the pupils for easy reference. Size, 6x9 inches. Cloth. Price (with 100 cards), 35 cents.

District-School Dialogues. By Marie Irish. A collection of twenty-five new, humorous dialogues for children of all ages. 160 pages. Paper. Price, 30 cents.

The Best Christmas Book. By Joseph C. Sindelar. Dialogues, recitations, songs, drills, pantomimes, tableaux, etc., for Christmas entertainment. 192 pages. Paper. Price, 30 cents.

Best Memory Gems. Selected and edited by Joseph C. Sindelar. Contains 400 of the choicest gems culled from the best in literature, and indexed by authors, by first lines, and by sentiment. For primary, intermediate and grammar grades. 64 pages. Paper. Price, 15 cents.

Best Primary Recitations. By Winifred A. Hoag. Over 200 original recitations for first and second grades. 88 pages. Paper. Price, 15 cents.

Best Primary Songs. By Amos M. Kellogg. Nearly sixty songs for primary and ungraded schools. 48 large pages. Paper. Price, 15 cents.

Merry Melodies. By S. C. Hanson. A book of school songs. Over one-half million copies already sold. 64 large pages. Paper. Price, 15 cents.

128-page illustrated Catalogue of Books mailed upon request

BECKLEY-CARDY COMPANY   Publishers   **CHICAGO**

CPSIA information can be obtained
at www.ICGtesting.com
Printed in the USA
BVHW061455260321
603434BV00001B/109